fashion worlds

The Deutsche Nationalbibliothek lists this publication in the Deutsche Nationalbibliografie; detailed bibliographical data are available on the internet at http://dnb.dnb.de

ISBN 978-3-03768-103-9
© 2012 by Braun Publishing AG
www.braun-publishing.ch

1st edition 2012

Selection of projects: Michelle Galindo, Manuela Roth
Text editing and translation: Judith Vonberg
Art direction: Michaela Prinz

michelle galindo

fashion
worlds

contemporary retail spaces

BRAUN

Content

1   2   3   4   5   6   7

8   9   10   11   12   13

14   15   16   17   18   19

above: Evolution of fashion from 1500–1880.
below: Johannes Schiess, Appenzell weaver couple at work on a hand loom, around 1830. Watercolor.

Fashion Worlds – Contemporary Retail Spaces
by Markus Hattstein

For as long as humans have lived in organized societies, clothing has represented far more than a simple means of protecting oneself from the cold or covering the body. It has always had a close and immutable relationship with ideas of self-expression, status and identity. At the same time, clothing has always been subject to changing fashions and trends, providing an easy means for individuals to compare themselves with others and make judgments on the basis of outward appearance. Attire in whatever form and context exists therefore in an arena fraught with tension, where the comfort of conformity confronts the possibility of individuality.

Fashion seeks to resolve this conflict by allowing individuals to both reveal and conceal themselves in the wearing of a particular garment, a garment that can also be an expression of self-image or mood, or of the individual's acceptance of a social role. These expressive elements exist alongside aesthetic ones – what will the wearer and what do others find appealing or attractive? Fashions have always been temporary and periodic – one speaks of fashion "waves" and "seasons" (the latter of which often correspond to seasons in nature), both of which imply correctly that trends and styles can experience revivals. An important question for researchers, designers and sellers of fashion concerns the influence or even the manipulation of taste: what is currently "in" and what defines individual expression as opposed to mass taste? Yet equally significant are questions such as: Who are the trendsetters? Who is creating new fashions? Who are the avant-garde and who are just the hangers-on? Fashion designers and fashion stores never leave these matters to chance, but rather employ targeted product placement and advertising to promote and sell their products, campaigns planned down to the smallest detail and orchestrated with military precision.

Early Developments

In the Middle Ages, the role of clothing as a means of distinguishing between genders and social ranks became particularly pronounced. While the lower classes often had to make do with homemade garments to serve their practical needs, spun or stitched together out of leather, hemp or sheep's wool, the upper classes clothed themselves in velvet, silk and other stylish fabrics, indulging in expensive fashions. By this time, production centers of high-end textiles had already become established, notably in Flanders and Northern Italy, catering for the moneyed elite of Europe, for whom particular fabrics and colors were reserved. Yet with the rise of the middle classes, the locus of creativity in the world of fashion began to shift: while attire for the nobility in the Ancien Régime was generally lavish and fussy for both sexes, a divergent trend emerged in around 1800 that persisted until the 1980s. While female fashion continued to become increasingly elaborate and flamboyant, male fashion, in contrast, became simpler and more restrained. Like the aristocratic class in earlier centuries, the middle classes left questions of style to the specialists: designers dreamt up fashionable trends and couturiers created individual garments.

In the course of their emancipation, the middle classes inherited not only fashion from the nobility, but also the tendency to separate work at home from gainful employment. This was a new freedom created by new prosperity that made it possible for the head of the household to be the sole breadwinner, while the wife or mother no longer needed to seek employment outside home. Among the lower classes, however, all family members including women and children had no choice but to work to earn money, often in an enterprise run from the home. An interesting exception to this general rule that divided the classes was the textile industry – this was a form of handicraft that even women of upper classes were happy to engage in. Almost all women could sew in those days, for

AU POLO
Robe d'après-midi de Worth

Gazette du Bon Ton. — Nº 4   *Juin 1913. — Pl. X*

sewing was a skill easily learned and with little operating expense. The production of clothes in the home beyond the requirements of the immediate family offered therefore an excellent opportunity to earn money, especially for young unmarried women in the lower classes. Since most of these women had no contacts in the industry, so-called "middle men" negotiated the sale of the products to wholesalers and clothing stores. These stores then sold the goods and passed customer feedback to the producers at work in their homes. After 1900, it became increasingly common to see women employed as salespeople in the womenswear departments of large stores, although they were still unable to rise to higher positions.

This system, involving individuals working from home sewing garments by hand, was surprisingly resistant to the mechanization sweeping through the rest of the textile industry in the first century after the Industrial Revolution. The first spinning machine was made in England in 1764, while 1785 saw the first fully mechanical loom. In 1805 the fully automatic Jacquard weaving loom was invented, and the spinning and weaving industries thereafter became subject to massive and rapid mechanization. Textile enterprises based in homes and small communities began to disintegrate. The artistic and highly individual creation of exclusive goods was replaced by the technically perfect mass production of identical garments. Factories were simply able to manufacture faster, cheaper and in greater quantities.

Sewing, however, remained mostly un-mechanized until after 1830 and, even then, the industry did not entirely lose its tradition of individual or one-off production. It was only in 1829 that the Frenchman Barthélemy Thimonnier (1793–1857) developed the first prototype for the modern sewing machine and established one of the first sewing machine factories in Paris, later burnt down by angry home workers. It took until 1870 before improved sewing

machine models appeared on the market, alongside new models for use in the home which became smaller and increasingly practical and portable in the decades that followed. In the meantime, home workers engaged in sewing garments were increasingly pressured to meet the demands of large textile houses, but new sewing machine models designed with such users in mind usually enabled them to do so. In 1900, there were already 200 sewing machine factories in Germany alone.

The Beginnings of the Fashion Boutique and Haute Couture

The fashion boutique began its rise during the second half of the 19th century, a period dominated by large department stores. In contrast to classic tailors, who produced individual pieces to order, fashion boutiques combined the broad selection of products offered by department stores with the more limited but specialized range found in specialty shops. While today's fashion stores usually focus on combining garments with shoes, belts, accessories and jewelry, pioneers of fashion stores and of haute couture were deliberate purists. Charles Frederick Worth (1826–1895), who emigrated from his native England to Paris, is generally acknowledged to be the founder of the fashion boutique and of haute couture; even today, partic-

left: Maurice Taquoy, Au Polo. Robe d'Après-Midi de Worth, 1913.
right: Franz Xaver Winterhalter, Portrait of the Empress Eugénie (1826–1920), 1853.

ular characteristics of such stores can be attributed to his influence. Worth came to Paris in 1845 and worked in the prestigious Maison Gagelin, a fashion store specializing in silk. There, he met and married Marie Vernet, who, at his suggestion, often modeled the boutique's new collections of scarves and hats. This revolutionary idea – using young, attractive women to model garments and accessories – became, as we well know, a vast and successful industry. Worth was not just an excellent tailor and salesman, but also a designer – in 1855 he won first prize at the International Exhibition in Paris for a coat of his own creation.

Soon after, Worth took the risk of venturing into the sale of finished garments, rather than just fabrics, despite the fact that the manufacture of clothing was regarded much less highly than the time-honored trade in fabric. Forced to become an independent tradesman, he found himself an investor (the Swede Otto Bobergh) and founded his own fashion house (Worth et Bobergh) in 1858 in the Parisian Rue de la Paix. Soon, customers began to request replicas of garments designed by himself and showcased by his wife and other models. In this period, he was also busy producing extravagant eveningwear for the wives of various diplomats, a fact noted by the Empress Eugénie, whose influence resulted in the appointment of Worth as official fashion purveyor to the court. Before long, he was designing unique garments for the British Queen Victoria and the Austrian Empress Elisabeth ("Sisi"), the latter of whom was a revered beauty and fashion icon for her time. In the famous painting of Sisi by Franz Xaver Winterhalter (1865), she can be seen wearing a dress designed by Worth. Worth's designs were revolutionizing the world of elegant female fashion – his dresses were much shorter than previous fashions had dictated, and flowing trains were eliminated entirely in favor of waist- and hemlines that accentuated the female figure. Worth's fashion house and designs had become leaders in haute couture; notable figures from all walks of life travelled long distances to Paris just to purchase one of Worth's garments. His clothes were so expensive that even wealthy patrons often came simply to have their Worth dress updated according to the latest fashion.

At the height of his fame, Worth did not simply design in response to the demands of his customers, but also followed his own creative path, presenting his newest creations four times a year at his own fashion show. Luxury pieces designed for specific seasons or even times of day, such as the "afternoon robe," were displayed at these events. Patrons who had travelled to see the show chose a garment and a fabric from those paraded in front of them, and Worth would then produce the item according to the individual's measurements. Worth's brand did not just set the tone for the high-end styles and fashions of

Franz Xaver Winterhalter, Empress Elisabeth in Courtly Gala Dress with Diamond Stars, 1865, oil on canvas.

his day – he had also built a fashion empire. By 1870 he employed more than 1,200 seamstresses, mostly as home workers, who produced many hundreds of garments every week. From 1867 onwards, he revolutionized his chain of distribution by producing paper patterns for buyers abroad. Worth perceived himself as a creator of fashion, more an artist of the imagination than a manual craftsman. To ensure the distinctiveness of his products, his name tag was sewn into every garment – an early, if concealed, form of brand logo. He was also one of the earliest designers of fashion to conceive his products as finished articles, rejecting any need to work with a milliner who would traditionally design accessories to complete the outfit.

Paris Remains the Center

Paris did not only have Worth to thank for the city's continued success as the center of haute couture and of the fashion boutique. The makers of fashion and managers of fashion houses, who expanded Worth's model of production and trade, also played a significant role. Jacques Doucet (1853–1929) ran a shop in Paris for exclusive, high-end female fashion in the finest materials, and was responsible for attiring many stars of the emerging medium of film, driving haute couture to increasingly lavish, imaginative and radical levels. As a prominent art collector and accepted authority on matters of taste, he also displayed works by the Impressionists and even the young Picasso in his salon, establishing a relationship between fashion, art and lifestyle that would persist into the 21st century.

Paul Poiret (1879–1944), mentored by Worth and Doucet, established his own female fashion house in 1904, primarily selling flowing robes influenced by oriental designs. Inspired by the trend in dress reform, he created the jupe-culotte and designed garments that could be worn without a corset, thereby taking the female fashion industry in an entirely new direction. In 1911 he introduced his own brand of perfume to the market, named after his daughter Rosine ("Parfums de Rosine") – the first of many designer perfumes created by a fashion brand. However, it was to be his fiercest rival, Coco Chanel, who would perfect this revolutionary concept and drive Poiret out of the market.

Countless legends have sprung up concerning the life of Coco Chanel (1883–1971), icon of haute couture in the early 20th century, legends which she herself encouraged. She was the first fashion designer to market not only her products, but also herself as a "brand." From working class roots, she rose rapidly in the emerging world of fashion, opening a hat shop in Paris in 1910 and her first fashion boutique just a year later. She soon established several further outlets in Biarritz, where she secured various

dress, Chanel was considered to have brought about the liberation of women from the corset, for which she was widely praised, despite the fact that her less successful rival Paul Poiret was perhaps more deserving of that claim. On the launch of the now world-renowned dress, Vogue described it as "a sort of uniform for all women of taste," implying that a mass-produced product could represent the height of elegance despite the established idea to the contrary. Chanel's fashion label was to produce not only extortionately priced individual pieces for film stars and aristocrats, but also tastefully manufactured garments for fashion-conscious women in the middle classes.

In the following years, Coco Chanel systematically constructed a fashion empire of previously unheard-of proportions. Using her connections with the German forces occupying France during the Second World War, she "Aryanized" her empire, divesting her Jewish financier Pierre Wertheimer of his share of the company. She was forced into exile in Switzerland in 1945, but returned to Paris in 1954, shortly afterwards introducing her "Chanel Suit" comprising a knitted wool cardigan and matching skirt. Worn mostly by increasingly self-confident business-women, the outfit enabled Chanel to re-connect almost seamlessly with her success of the pre-war years. Her brand name was by now fully established, along with her designer perfume "Chanel No 5," first marketed in 1923, and the now world-famous brand logo – the interlaced double "C" in sober black and white. Coco Chanel, who continued to design collections until her death and even stage-managed her own funeral procession of models wearing Chanel outfits, was the sole female representative from the fashion industry in Time Magazine's list of the 100 most influential people of the 20th century.

After Chanel's death, her brand struggled to keep pace with the fashion industry, becoming known for its collections for rich, elderly ladies rather than modern, sophisticated women. This changed again, however, when Karl Lagerfeld took on a role as designer for the Chanel brand.

The existence of a second "fashion tsar", whose collection contrasted Chanel's in many ways, guaranteed that Paris was renewed as the center both of haute couture and of fashion boutiques from 1947 onwards, once the years of war and post-war austerity that had temporarily allowed New York to become the center of the fashion world were over. This tsar was Christian Dior (1905–1957). Educated as a draughtsman in the fashion industry, he opened a fashion boutique in 1946 in the Parisian Avenue Montaigne (still the brand's flagship store today) and launched a radical ultra-feminine "New Look" at his first fashion show in February 1947. Combining flared skirts and corseted bodices with an emphasis on the female

wealthy patrons as financial backers. In contrast to her predecessors and competitors, she was successful in her attempt to liberate haute couture from the taste for impractical opulence and prettiness that continued to inhibit its development. Instead, she created a simple and functional but elegant style of female fashion using jersey (a cotton-based material) and sharp lines to create athletic garments that allowed easy movement and accentuated the female form. By 1916, she had more than 300 seamstresses in her employ, and by 1936 her fashion empire had created 4,000 jobs. Through seeking out and establishing relationships with a range of public figures from artists to aristocrats, Chanel was able to use the free media exposure that these personalities attracted to bring her products into the public eye. Many later fashion designers noted this strategy and used it themselves to great effect. Furthermore, she cultivated excellent contacts with leading fashion magazines, frequently launching new designs in their pages where they were declared to be setting the standard for haute couture, thus establishing her brand throughout the fashion world as the epitome of modern elegance.

In 1926 Coco Chanel introduced her famous "little black dress" to the world in the magazine Vogue, which in 1916 had declared Coco Chanel's designs to represent the epitome of elegance. The dress, which would later become famous as the cocktail dress of the 1950s and 1960s, was short (never falling below the knee) and appropriate for a range of different occasions. In designing the

left: Cynthia Rowley spring 2007 show,
New York Fashion Week.
right: Chanel Haute Couture Fall-Winter 2011–2012
Fashion Show held at Grand Palais in Paris.

waist, Dior named the look "Corolle" (literally "corolla" or "circlet of flower petals"). In defiance of all his critics, Dior had recognized that female fashion was in desperate need of a more luxurious and carefree style after years of enforced adversity and restraint. Moreover, the very feminine, impractical "New Look" endorsed the classic, conservative conception of gender roles in 1950s and early 1960s USA and Europe.

Not only did Dior encourage the trend for affordable fashion chains and mass-produced garments, enabling the woman on the street to wear clothes inspired by the Dior style, but he also granted licenses worldwide, allowing firms to manufacture his garments. This practice eventually became the standard business model of leading fashion houses. Dior went further and extended his license to cosmetics, stockings and fashion accessories, becoming in the process something of a fashion dictator. In the following years, he introduced a new look with every new season, taken up at first by his wealthy patrons as well as every female monarch and president's wife, then by the entire fashion industry: the "Zig Zag" line, the "Lily of the Valley" line, the pencil skirt, the A-line, the H-line, the Y-line, and so on.

By 1947, Dior had already launched his first designer perfume ("Miss Dior"), the beginning of a global perfume empire alongside his empire of fashion. Dior's custom of incorporating leading designers and couturiers into his empire, allowing them to create with very few stipulations or inhibitions, was hugely lucrative, but also sowed the seeds for later rivalries. Suffering a heart attack at the height of his fame, Dior was succeeded as head designer by his assistant Yves Saint-Laurent (1936–2008), who shortly afterwards launched his own independent fashion house, competing against the Dior brand in the haute couture market. With his "Ligne Trapèze," Saint-Laurent freed women from wasp waists and stiff supports at the waist, bosom and shoulders, while retaining a certain Dior-inspired elegance. His designs contributed significantly to the new paths being pursued in the world of fashion during the 1960s – his feminine trouser suit "Le Smoking" (1967), the beatnik look, tweed suits, tight trousers and thigh-high boots all combined the concepts of emancipation and femininity, the two key ideas at the center of the 1960s revolutions, with something intriguingly androgynous. In later years, he maintained his reputation as a trend-setter with styles such as the "Nostalgia Look" and

the "Rich Peasant" or "Peasant Chic" look, as well as his perfume "Opium" (1977), which became one of the most successful scents worldwide, and his brand logo "YSL," one of the most recognizable logos of any international company. In 1999 the Yves Saint-Laurent brand was bought by the Gucci Group (now the PPR Group).

Haute Couture and Prêt-à-porter

Despite their undeniable success, the Parisian fashion boutiques were unable to prevent the growth of fashion stores and chains worldwide that began to threaten their market dominance. Even after the First World War, and to a much greater extent after the Second, the democratization of society ushered in a new era and industry of widespread mass culture and entertainment, serving a society that, on the surface at least, was experiencing a gradual leveling of classes and ranks. New fashion houses sprang up to meet the new demand not only for mass-produced products that would satisfy mass tastes, but also for fashionable new trends that would be available to a far broader clientele than Parisian haute couture.

Since the 19th century, France's fashion empires had sought to protect their exclusivity – in 1868 the leading fashion designers in Paris had joined forces to create the alliance known today as Chambre Syndicale de la Haute Couture, which had also supported an exclusive fashion school since 1927. (It is interesting to note that corresponding chambers for Prêt-à-porter and male fashion were established only in 1973.) This body formulated strict, yet regularly amended criteria concerning the admittance of a fashion house or chain into their federation. The firm must have its headquarters in Paris, have a fixed number of permanent employees, produce at least 35 (reduced from 50) different unique pieces for day and eveningwear, each created by hand and by an accredited fashion designer ("Grand Couturier"), and hold a public fashion show in Paris every season (twice a year). Since 1997, a few non-French firms – Valentino, Armani and Versace – have been invited to join as accredited fashion houses and since 2001 as correspondent members, permitted to exhibit their designs and offered the possibility of becoming full members in the future. After 1945, there were at times more than 100 firms registered as members of the haute couture federation; by 1990 this had fallen to 20 and in 2011 there were just 15. The haute couture fashion shows no longer serve simply as a

above: Afghan employees working at a
contemporary textile factory.
below: Zara Flagship Store in Rome, Italy.

means of displaying each firm's best pieces to the other members, but also of parading their best-selling products and brand logos in front of the international press.

The democratization of both fashion and taste was due in no small part to the highly visible array of fashion and women's magazines that emerged in all developed countries after the Second World War, with their fashion tips and ubiquitous advertising of products aimed at the ordinary woman. With this development, the phrase "off the rack" quickly lost its earlier, distasteful association with cheap, mass-produced garments designed purely for convenience.

This new type of fashion – becoming known as Prêt-à-porter or ready-to-wear – covered the whole spectrum of price, from value products to high-end garments, and a spectrum of fashion, from everyday wear to sophisticated extravagance. Many fashion houses – even a few haute couture firms or chains – produce their own Prêt-à-porter product lines, often manufactured en masse in industrial production processes, but sometimes still created by hand in limited numbers and for a limited time period. They are, however, never one-off pieces and are generally bought as finished garments in standard sizes, although they are often exhibited at fashion shows as if they were unique pieces. It quickly became common practice for firms and products in the Prêt-à-porter sector to sell licenses or the fashion items themselves in other countries, as well as locating the manufacturing processes – at least the initial stages of the process – in third world or developing countries where large amounts of cheap labor could be found.

Fashion Chains and their Channels of Distribution

The fashion chains of the Prêt-à-porter industry are now ubiquitous in the inner-city areas of large metropolises in industrialized countries. The design of their stores, reproduced in every outlet throughout a country, a continent, or even the world, ensures a strong brand identity, while also giving rise to complaints concerning the increasing homogeneity and lack of variety in shopping malls and streets over the world. To remain competitive in the lowest price sectors, the goods manufactured by these firms must be mass-produced rapidly and cheaply, hence the tendency to use cheap labor in Eastern Europe, Asia, Latin America or Africa. Currently, most such garments are manufactured in Asia, before being transported thousands of kilometers by ship to Europe or North America, and often hundreds of kilometers to their final destination on the shelves, a process that is usually much more economical than the cost of manufacturing the products in the countries in which they are eventually sold. It is interesting to note that certain elements of today's global textile industry echo the

conditions of production that were prevalent in Europe in the 19th and early 20th centuries. In the third world countries where garments are manufactured, it is often young, unmarried women who work in textile factories or at home to produce goods for export according to standard patterns. Native middlemen or franchises also play a decisive, although often dubious, role in the production and distribution of the products.

Although the outsourcing of production and global chains of distribution are perhaps an obvious result of the processes of globalization, these practices would not be so prevalent without vast social and economic disparities across the globe. Manufacture in low-wage countries often fails to meet the standards of pay, employment law, health and safety, representation of workers' interests (through trade unions, workers' councils, wage negotiations, etc.) or welfare provision required in industrialized nations – and that is without even touching on environmental concerns. In the context of increasingly vociferous international protests against social injustices and inequality, these glaring disparities regularly provoke criticism and even anger, and have led to various trade and production agreements within the textile industry to ensure minimum international standards. In industrialized nations, too, increasing numbers of consumers are demanding that transnational companies pay greater attention to issues such as human rights, hygiene and welfare standards and the ecological impact of production and distribution, for example, calling for a ban on child labor, still common in textile manufacturing in several countries.

Until the 1980s, the idea of "fair trade" in the textile industry would have been dismissed as the utopian fantasy of a few ecologically minded dreamers. Yet, since the 1990s, the movement for fairly traded clothing, guaranteeing a minimum wage for the producers, emphasizing sustainable development and building relationships between producer and consumer countries based on a cooperative model, has become a significant economic factor, controlled by various organizations according to strict criteria. In 1997, the FLO (Fairtrade Labelling Organizations International) was founded as the umbrella organization for commerce coming under the remit of "Fairtrade," and 2001 saw the publication of a set of guidelines for the production of Fairtrade goods.

Logos and Branding

By the 1980s, a wide range of transnational fashion companies were contributing to the development of new trends, although a few individual fashion houses had emerged as global leaders, conducting frequent mergers with firms in other sectors to further increase their market share. This was not only beneficial to the large companies, but also enabled smaller brands and fashion producers, catering to niche markets and subcultures, to expand and develop. A growing "Body Culture", focusing the attention of individuals on the cultivation of self image, shaping an identity through their outward appearance, also had the effect of heightening consumers' brand consciousness. Furthermore, many fashion designers felt newly liberated to experiment with new ideas of gender and body image, designing collections suitable for emerging, sometimes radical, lifestyles – adjectives such as classy or chic were now joined by endearing, funky and garish. Fashion was now being mediated primarily through visual media, from style icons such as Madonna and Princess Diana to TV series such as Miami Vice, where the apparently effortless class of the fashion on display was a key factor in the show's appeal.

With help from market and consumer analysts, many fashion companies began to establish a cult image around their logo and indeed their entire brand that was at least as potent as that surrounding their actual products. Not only was the logo increasingly a key element in the company's ability to shape its identity, but it also ensured that the brand was memorable, distinctive and easily recognizable. Most successful brand logos were designed according to the acronym "KISS" – Keep It Short (and) Simple. A few leading fashion houses commissioned notable artists and designers to create their logos, although several were forced to undergo lengthy and often highly contentious lawsuits to ensure patent protection.

Fashion companies were equally scientific and systematic when it came to branding – the process of managing a brand through the creation and development both of the brand and of the products themselves. This involves a delicate balancing act between the preservation of a tried and tested brand on which customers can rely and a readiness to adapt rapidly to and even to initiate new trends, enabling the brand to attract new customers. The brand image must remain closely in touch with the demands of the existing consumer base in order to be sure of their continued custom, while also continuing to develop and modernize. Acceptance and recognizability must be balanced with innovation and surprise. Since the 1980s, almost all fashion companies and chains have sought to maintain this balance with line extensions: they begin as fashionable clothing companies before quickly diversifying into accessories, shoes, perfume or lifestyle products sold under the same logo (often through franchises). The aim is to ensure that customers can have their every demand met by a single brand, which therefore becomes synonymous with a particular way of life. In today's world, where the vast array of fashion houses or chains and their products is impossible to ignore, it is often no longer the fashion item itself that distinguishes between brands, but the brand, its logo and the particular way of life it represents.

A Few Examples

There are many notable fashion houses and chains that have influenced the world of fashion outside the field of French haute couture, some of which have become leaders in very specific sectors. The few that have been chosen for discussion here represent just a small selection of these influential fashion houses.

Alongside France, Italy became a world leader in the design and production of high-end fashion, for which Milan is still renowned worldwide. In 1921, the Florentine Guccio Gucci (1881–1953) opened a shop for leather goods and equestrian supplies, which he turned into a fashion and jewelry enterprise in 1947. Since the 1970s, the Gucci concern has been known and admired internationally and the interwoven Gs of this vast empire's logo are recognizable worldwide.

Giorgio Armani (born 1943) established a menswear store in Milan in 1974, which he soon expanded to incorporate womenswear and later underwear and swimwear. In 1982 he created the now famous perfume "Armani." He favored discreet, monotone fabrics and is noted for inventing the color "greige" – a mixture of grey and beige. The billion-dollar, transnational fashion house with a stylized eagle for its logo now boasts more than 500 boutiques in 46 countries.

Gianni Versace (1946–1997) was a supremely creative fashion designer who opened his first shop in Milan in 1979. Under the brand logo of Medusa, he created a variety of collections from jeans to spectacular stage costumes. Since his assassination in 1997 the fashion chain has been managed by his sister Donatella (born 1955), now head designer.

The firm Benetton was founded in 1965 by four siblings in Ponzano Veneto (Northern Italy) and has remained under the management of the same family until today. Developing various fashion labels for different target groups, the firm has also made a name for itself as a key sponsor of motor racing. The distinctive logo – "United Colors of Benetton" written on a green background – was thrust into the public eye during an aggressive advertizing campaign that used shocking images of AIDS victims, death row inmates and war victims through which the company sought to "tear down the wall of indifference." The blood-stained hand of a war victim positioned under the brand logo caused a particular outcry.

UNITED COLORS
OF BENETTON.

Supports
the Unhate Foundation
unhatefoundation.org

SUPREME LEADER OF NORTH KOREA

PRESIDENT OF SOUTH KOREA

left: Poster of a United Colors of Benetton Campaign, 2010.
right: Shopping arcade Galleria Vittorio Emanuele II in Milan.

Prada, originally a luxury leather goods firm founded in 1913 in Milan by two brothers, is today recognized around the world by its distinctive logo – a triangle balanced on its point. Under the management of Minuccia Prada (born 1949) since the 1980s, the brand has become accepted as a world leader, not only in high-quality leather goods, but also in luxurious and elegant fashion accessories, as a result of the concern's successful diversification into sunglasses, perfume and the female fashion collection "Miu Miu" launched in 1993. Films such as "The Devil Wears Prada" have further contributed to the brand's position as a global leader, although Prada's strong brand identity has also encouraged the production of and trade in imitation Prada products, most notably in Asia.

One of the greatest success stories is that of Calvin Klein (born 1942), an American who set up his fashion company in 1968, expanding into perfumes and watches in the 1970s. Sold to an American shirt manufacturer in 2002, the brand is reputedly worth around $34.7 billion today, making it the most prosperous fashion company in the world.

Among German fashion houses, Jil Sander's enterprise, founded in Hamburg in 1968 for chaste, restrained styles of womenswear, is still a leading light in the field. In 1997 the company launched a menswear range and just two years later, the concern was bought by Prada. Wolfgang Joop (born 1944) is noted for his striking creativity, which first garnered attention in 1982 with the launch of his womenswear range, followed soon after by a men's collection in 1985, as well as designs for Meissen porcelain. In 1999 he was the co-founder of "Wunderkind GmbH" for high-end female fashion. In 1973, Gerhard Weber founded the firm Gerry Weber (operating under this name since

1986) in Halle (Westphalia), designing and producing womens- and menswear, shoes and fashion accessories. The chain now has more than 300 outlets, sells its products through more than 6000 franchises and in 2001 was listed on the MDAX (German stock index).

The Swedish corporation H&M (Hennes & Mauritz), founded in 1947 and starting to trade under its current name in 1968 after a merger, is represented today in every large inner city in Western and Central Europe, trading in over 2,300 stores worldwide, 350 of which are in Germany. Large chains such as H&M are often reproached for their contribution to the increasing homogeneity of the retail segments of inner cities. H&M seeks to reduce this impact by launching unique collections such as the Karl Lagerfeld range in 2004 or the high-end range "Collection of Style" (COS), but continues to attract criticism for the working conditions of its foreign employees. In 2007, the company was widely condemned for using child labor to transport cotton out of Uzbekistan and in 2010, a further outcry was caused when news of the low wages of garment producers in Bangladesh was made public. H&M responded to public pressure by declaring its willingness to abide by certain standards and regulations.

Lacoste, with its well-known green crocodile logo and more than 1,100 boutiques worldwide, is an example of a successful firm that has remained within a small sector of the market. The French tennis player René Lacoste (1904–1996) designed and made a polo shirt for himself in 1927 which he began to mass produce in 1933. From the 1960s onwards, Lacoste found itself as a market leader in sport and leisure clothing, cultivating an image of both effortless class and simple athleticism through its distinctive products.

» A **woman** should **get dressed every day** as if she could meet her **great love.** «

Coco Chanel

24 Issey Miyake

Hakata Fukuoka, Japan

Architect: Hisaaki Hirawata +
Tomohiro Watabe /
Moment Design
Year of completion: 2011
Gross floor area: 79 m²
Materials: vinyl tile (floor),
AEP painting (walls and
ceiling), corian / powder
coated painting on steel
(table)

Somewhat unusually, the designers of 24 conceived the fashion boutique as a convenience store, where customers are invited to browse a wide range of Issey Miyake goods in a casual atmosphere. Without the products there would be no store, so it is the products themselves that exist as the central design element. Their vibrancy provides the color that draws the eye, while visitors add the movement that brings the space to life. Transparent spheres wrap and contain while not obscuring the goods – indeed, the longer one looks, the more the structure itself recedes, leaving only the multicolored garments. This is a store that manifests the ultimate in understatement.

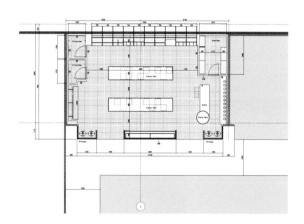

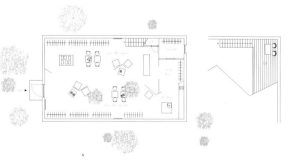

5²
Shizuoka, Japan

Architect: Suppose Design Office
Year of completion: 2011
Gross floor area: 127 m²
Materials: metal sheet, concrete and glass

Natural light pours into the interior of this fashion boutique designed by Japanese architects Suppose Design Office, casting outerwear, shoes and other outdoor products in a natural glow that is appropriate for their purpose. The recessed skylight illuminates a gallery of hanging coats, shirts and trousers. A zigzagging metal wall divides this area from a display of undergarments, jerseys and accessories, indoor products lit by warm artificial lighting from light bulbs dangling from the ceiling. A staircase in one corner leads to a first-floor mezzanine overlooking the shop floor. The simplicity of this design belies the innovative, even radical display methods on show.

Alter Shop

Shanghai, China

Architect: 3Gatti Architecture Studio
Year of completion: 2010
Gross floor area: 100 m²
Materials: steel structure, concrete bricks, white terrazzo cement, wax, plasterboard, grey cement, epoxy, plywood, leather

Sonja Long had a radical vision for the interior of her fashion store in Shanghai, a vision encompassing inverted values, alternative beauties and subverted points of view. Inspired by Sonja's unconventional ideas, Francesco Gatti produced a striking design that would render those ideas concrete. A stair surface covers the office and fitting rooms, lending additional shape and form to the small interior and providing a means to exhibit the high-end products in a multidimensional way. The philosophy of Alter is to both be and inspire an alternative world, one in which the rules of the real everyday world no longer apply, a world reminiscent of Escher's, where space and shape are molded in new and fascinating ways.

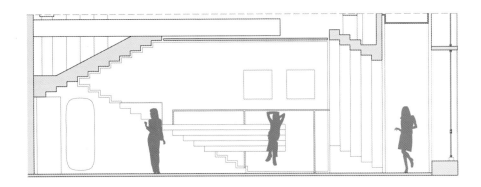

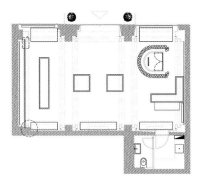

Arzu Kaprol Gallery

Istanbul, Turkey

Architect: Autoban
Year of completion: 2010
Gross floor area: 70 m²
Materials: carrara marble, tiles, painted iron, lacquered wooden, stainless steel

Situated in Istanbul's Galata district, an area heavily densely populated with art galleries and specialized shops, Turkey's respected fashion designer Arzu Kaprol displays her collections in a spectacular but understated renovated historical building known as "Kamondo Inn." Autoban conserved the original brick arc structure of the space, complementing it by building around it in order to expose the rough yet beautiful architectural shell and

strengthening the dramatic effect with reciprocal mirrors. A celebrated piece from Autoban's recent collection, "Reedy Bookcases," is customized and embedded inside the arcs, while precious carrara marble is perfectly employed for the display cases and storage units. Shadows cast by lighting entice the visitor to engage with this uniquely designed space.

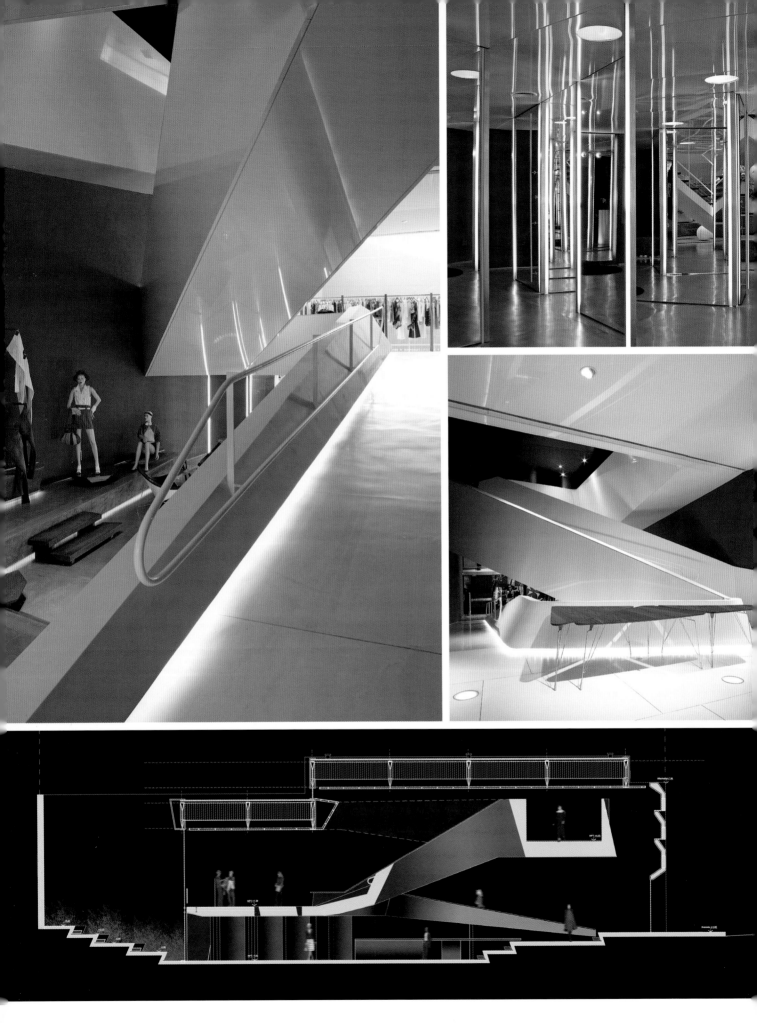

Ayres

Buenos Aires, Argentina

Architect: Dieguez Fridman
Arquitectos & Asociados
Year of completion: 2008
Gross floor area: 480 m²
Materials: zinc sheeting
(façade), Lapacho wood, mir-
rors glass, Barrisol, concrete
(floor)

Just as cities are perceived and explored in motion, offering unexpected encounters and new perspectives with every glance, so does this interior replicate the feelings and sensations generated by urban space – there are surprises around every corner to reward the curious visitor. The basic element is a bright white object that unfolds in curved and diagonal lines inside the dark box of walls, floor and roof. Fitting rooms form a mesmerizing labyrinth of mirrors where clothes can be viewed from unusual angles, turning the experience of trying on clothes into an infinite game of shoppers, clothes and space. Diagonal openings in the zinc façade, a new material in the urban landscape of the Palermo district, hint at the space behind and invite exploration.

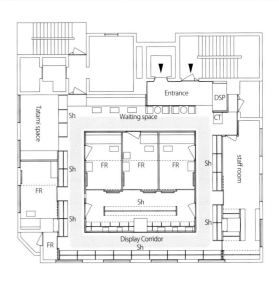

Bridal Magic

Himeji, Japan

Architect: Process5 Design / Tao Thong Villa
Lighting design: Ushio Inc., Mariko Hayashi
Year of completion: 2010
Gross floor area: 184 m²
Materials: milk pine flooring (NOSTAMO), tatami wall, mirrored panels, split stone (Advan), lacquered oak

Process5 Design have completed the interior of this classy bridal shop in Himeji, Japan. Called Bridal Magic, the store's key feature is a series of mirrored panels surrounding the changing rooms, randomly inlaid with frames. Some frames simply enclose mirrors, while others display accessories or contain apertures, lighting equipment or handles for the fitting room doors. End-

lessly reflecting the rails of dresses lining the store's walls, the mirrors create a fairytale bridal world through which each newly dressed bride steps, fresh from the fitting room in her beautiful gown. Just as it should be, this dazzling but understated store ensures that the bride remains the center of attention.

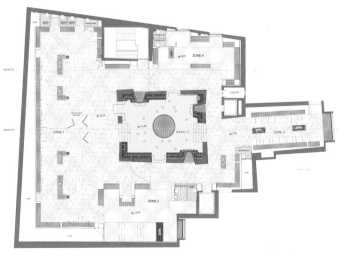

Candido 1859

Maglie-Lecce, Italy

Architect: LOLA
Year of completion: 2010
Gross floor area: 627 m²
Materials: (floor) ceramic, (wall) plasterboard, laminated glass ceiling

Candido 1859 is one of the first fashion label stores to open in Southern Italy. The Men's department consists of a main commercial area; three separated mono label spaces, and a "private" sales room and a storage area. This floor was a later addition to the original 18th century building that was formerly a private residence whose structure is characterized by thick walls and high vaulted ceilings. The challenge was to give a contemporary over-

haul to this structurally marginalized space characterized by a very low ceiling and a central patio covering the lower main entrance hall. The patio was raised to create the "private" sales room and its central round table with a reflective glass top works as a skylight for the lower spaces, offering an extra value to the entrance on the ground floor.

Capsula Multibrand Store

Budapest, Hungary

Architect: Göske Project
Year of completion: 2011
Gross floor area: 230 m²
Materials: marble surface plate and epoxy (floor), polymer foil (Barrisol sealing), high tempered glass, and high polished paint on wood and on plasterboard (walls)

The result of an intuitive and fruitful collaboration between the owner and two Hungarian architects, the new Capsula Multibrand Store is a stunning and elegant space located on an iconic boulevard in Budapest. As an "exhibition space" for limited edition and unique fashion pieces, it is the first of its kind in the city and combines urban contemporary design with traditional heritage elements. The interior space is resolved without barriers into a single open space where materials, furnishings, ornamentation and products are unified in a dramatic and monochromatic visual statement. The garments take center stage in front of a backdrop of glossy white surfaces and bold curving structures. Shiny barrisol folia provide the finish for the ceiling, a wispy reflective material that contrasts the strong black steel columns that support it.

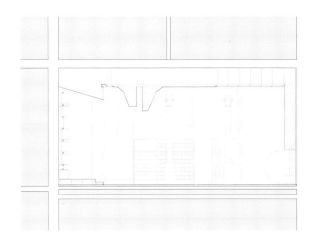

Cornet Boutique

Kumagaya, Japan

Architect: Kazutoyo Yamamoto / Dessence
Year of completion: 2010
Gross floor area: 107 m²
Materials: reinforced concrete, stone partitions

This unique boutique interior in Japan designed by Kazutoyo Yamamoto of Japanese Studio Dessence is filled with stone partitions with arched doorway openings. Full-height mirrors placed between the archways on the walls of the Cornet Boutique create the illusion of an infinite line of stone structures, of a town or even a city of garments mingling with architectural elements.

Fitting rooms are located centrally for easy access and tables have been incorporated into the layout, offering spaces for visitors to rest and relax in this urbanized fashion boutique, a welcome respite from a savage exterior world.

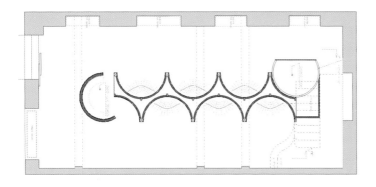

Creo

Mumbai, India

Architect: Sameep Padora and Associates
Year of completion: 2011
Gross floor area: 88 m²
Materials: cast acrylic, mild steel tube structure, in-situ epoxy floor

Designed by Indian firm Sameep Padora & Associates, the retail store Creo is located within a heritage building in Kemps Corner, Mumbai's premium shopping district. Redefining the brand's identity, as well as respecting the existing space, the designers detached the previous displays from the shell and replaced them with a dramatic free-standing installation which integrates an ingenious new display system. Generating an intimate customer experience, the centerpiece structure is subdivided into semi-circular niches creating an elegant chalice-shaped section. A white cast resin and acrylic skin covers the interior's complex curved geometrics, providing a blank canvas on which to showcase the vibrant array of products and clothing.

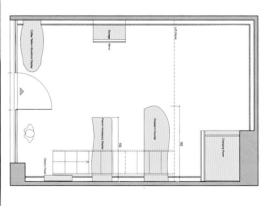

Delicatessen

Tel Aviv, Israel

Architect: Z-A studio
Year of completion: 2009
Gross floor area: 34 m²
Materials: pegboard (wall display), recycled furniture pieces

This two-story interior store is lined up with custom-perforated white hardboard, rejecting the elevated linoleum of the original boutique. Treating architecture like fashion and using cheap materials with sophistication, Zucker draped pegboard over the five meter high walls and lit the surface from behind, turning the crude material into a lace-like garment that graphically wraps the diminutive space. Accessorizing the grid of holes are hooks that evoke the image of a sewing pattern and provide day-to-night dressing, functioning as a display for clothes and, when bare, as an ornamental element. Complementing the vertical tailoring, striking horizontal furniture seems cut from the pegboard pattern and lifted off the wall to reveal a lemon-yellow "undergarment."

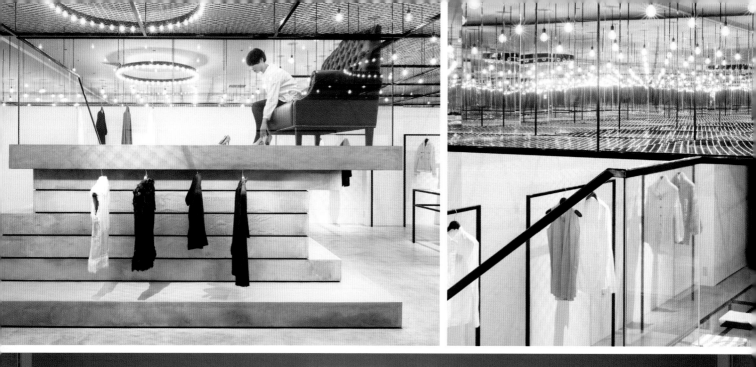

DURAS

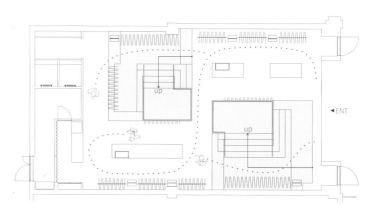

DURAS Daiba

Tokyo, Japan

Architect: Chikara Ohno / sinato
Year of completion: 2009
Gross floor area: 127 m²
Materials: mortar (floor), expanded metal (ceiling), mirror (walls)

The 3.65 meters-high ceiling of this boutique presented the designers with challenges as well as the stimulating opportunity to conceive and create a truly three-dimensional interior that privileges volume above surface. In response, a false ceiling made of expanded metal was added at 2.25 meters and a stepped platform inserted that invites shoppers up to a stunning attic space. Further stepped platforms are used to display bags, shoes and garments, lifting them above floor level and creating a spatially unique shopping experience for every customer. Mirrors positioned around the edge of the attic succeed in visually expanding the interior, which, to the unaccustomed eye, becomes an infinite all-encompassing monochromatic space that dazzles with its understated glamour.

Entrance Concept Store

Bucharest, Romania

Architect: Square One
Year of completion: 2009
Gross floor area: 200 m²
Materials: MDF polyurethane painted, custom made light system, plaster walls, aluminum structure

Jagged display stands and a network of black electrical cables dominate this monochromatic interior. The shapes and positions of the objects within the space were designed so as to create a maze of possible routes through the store – each visit results in a unique and enthralling architectural experience. Lightbulbs weighted at the ends of the black wires create mesmerizing angular lines fanning out over the ceiling and add warmth and light to the stark aesthetic. Further light is emitted from the sides of the angular stands, thus illuminating the merchandise. To wander through this space is to take a walk in a surreal pathless forest with a tangled canopy of branches overhead filtering the light, while unique plants and animals are met with at every turn – this space is like no other you will ever inhabit.

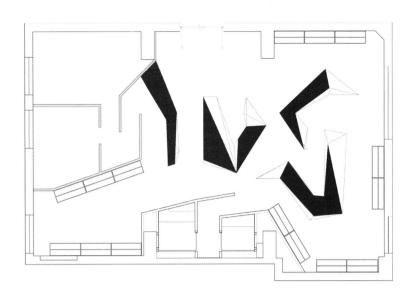

» I don't design clothes.
I design dreams. «
Ralph Lauren

Esprit Lighthouse Store

Cologne, Germany

Architect: Reich und Wamser
Year of completion: 2011
Gross floor area: 550 m²
Materials: american walnut, birch wood, oak, black steel, glass

Guiding the visitor back in time, back to the origins of Esprit at its conception in California, the interior of this Cologne store represents both a new and a cozily familiar architectural vision for the brand. Exposed brick walls, exquisitely crafted walnut display cabinets and tables, and gauzy curtains generate a homely feel that invites relaxed browsing. A courtyard-like room at the heart of the store is filled with plants, flowers and natural light that bathes the whole interior in a warm glow. At the rear of the shop, translucent white curtains conceal fitting rooms where charming lampshades resemble upturned woven baskets. Stepping inside this unassuming store feels like the warm embrace of an old friend – you feel at home and cannot resist the urge to stay a while.

Fame Agenda Docklands

Melbourne, Australia

Architect: Matt Gibson Architecture + Design
Year of completion: 2009
Materials: OSB panelling, mirrors, black glossy paint (walls)

Inspired by concepts of transparency and illusion, this store plays with customers' expectations of interior and exterior. A random and organic set of arches inspired by Thomas Hetherwick's sculptural works merge to form a cave-like enclosure from within the confines of the rectilinear shell. Partially covering existing structural piers and terminating with mirrored cladding behind the sales counter, generating an illusion of space, these arches create an intimate space, protected from the wind-blown Docklands promenade, while also providing merchandizing benches, walls and ceiling. Rudimentary materials are combined with the black satin paint of the background walls – a successful juxtaposition of homely warmth and sophistication that establishes a strong and unforgettable visual statement.

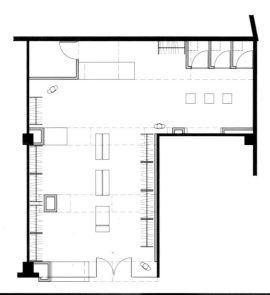

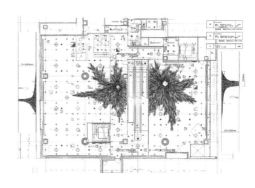

Fantastique Canopée

Tokyo, Japan

Architect: CoudamyDesign
Year of completion: 2012
Gross floor area: 125 m²
Materials: wood

Paul Coudamy's new sculptural fixture installed in a department store in Tokyo comprises 9,715 planks of wood that seem to grow out of the floor, rising and spreading to form two vast sheltering structures covering the ceiling. This modernist version of a wooden cave was constructed randomly, the placement of each plank the result of a spontaneous decision allowing the dynamic and unpredictable final structure to emerge. The chaotic yet strangely harmonious central sculpture is complemented by the neutral white walls and carefully positioned clothing displays. Every angle offers a new and dynamic perspective on the store's central element, a wooden sea filled with watery energy that celebrates the intimate relationship between nature and architecture.

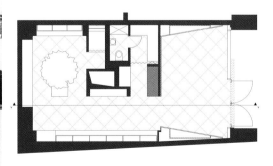

Firmament

Berlin, Germany

Architect: Paul Bauer & Efe Erenler in collaboration with Dirk Bonn
Year of completion: 2010
Gross floor area: 68 m²
Materials: regional walnut wood, travertine, drywall

Dirk Bonn and ErenlerBauer have recently redesigned a ground-floor space in a Roger Bundschuh building in central Berlin for Firmament, a high-end street-wear apparel store. The key idea was to make the shop window area a means of communicating with the passing public. Enlarged and created as a cone shape that opens up to the street, it functions as an innovative three-dimensional playground for a range of vibrant installations. In a radical twist on conventional shop windows, visitors are invited to not only look at, but to participate in the display by walking through it to enter the store. The regional walnut wood used for the traditional grid and the travertine floor were chosen for their links to traditional regional craftsmanship, ensuring that this store maintains a relationship with the past while also setting new trends for the future.

Folk Clothing, Brick Lane

London, United Kingdom

Architect: IYA Studio
Year of completion: 2010
Gross floor area: 93 m²
Materials: reclaimed wood, vintage furniture

Folk joined forces with IYA Studio to design this vast new store in a trendy East London location. The interior contains echoes of Folk's flagship store in North London while also exuding its own very distinct personality. Crafted wooden paneling, beautifully produced by Dougal Linnett and Evan Schwarz, was juxtaposed with clean white walls and simple clothing systems to create a quirky atmosphere. Marble heads designed by acclaimed sculptor Paul Van Stone provide a novel approach to seating, while a carefully selected range of vintage items including gym horses are used ingeniously for both seating and display. This interior offers many reasons to be excited about the ongoing collaboration between Folk and IYA Studio.

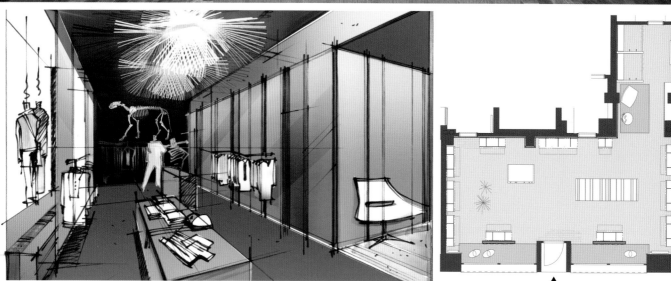

Geometry

Berlin, Germany

Architect: plajer & franz studio
Year of completion: 2008
Gross floor area: 100 m²
Materials: mud colored wall, wooden floors, brushed white oak furniture

With the design motto "How weird can you get," designers from plajer & franz studio created a store environment for Geometry conceived as the ideal residence for a crazy professor – one with good taste combined with an affection for obscure collections, such as photos of skeletons or lamps that look like jackstraws. Mud-colored walls, dark wooden floors and brushed white oak furniture exude elegance and sophistication, while the waiting areas with rugs and sputnik lamps create a home-like respite within the boutique.

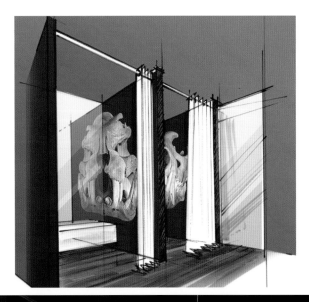

H&M

Barcelona, Spain

Architect: Estudio Mariscal
Other creatives: iGuzzini
(lighting design), Artecc
(renovation)
Year of completion: 2008
Gross floor area: 1,720 m²
Materials: original wood and
stone, LED screens, steel, glass

A 19th–century building, listed as a vestige of the bourgeois architecture and the work of Domènech Estapà, now houses an H&M shop. The architects made the effort to reform the building, highlight the aspects which, over time and the different uses of the building in its latest stage, had been removed or altered. The dome, the three public rooms, the staircase well and the imperial staircase were kept. The interior design is composed of features that can be added and removed. A second exempt skin was superimposed on the old architecture, creating a new image without blurring the original. This, which could have been an obstacle throughout the project, became an incentive as it finally helped the designers to achieve a multipurpose space which is flexible, modular and versatile.

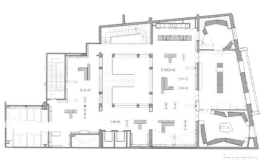

Hermès Rive Gauche

Paris, France

Architect: RDAI
Year of completion: 2010
Gross floor area: 2,155 m²
Materials: ash wood, mosaic tiles (floor, staircase, and columns), LED lights

Built in a swimming pool, Hermès Boutique Fashion represents a unique and radical reinterpretation of an existing space. Preserving the pool and the three large skylights that flood the interior with natural light, RDAI embraced the immense empty volume with its compelling Art Déco architectonic character. Heritage and modernity, savoir-faire and creation – the core values of Hermès – come alive in the transformation of this historic space, in which the only major modification was the introduction of concrete composite floor slabs supported by a light structure. A discreet façade gives onto an entrance that evokes an overturned lightwell, drawing one's gaze irrevocably towards the light-filled swimming pool, now inhabited by four dramatic wooden "huts" that house the Hermès collection.

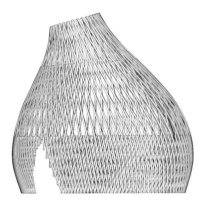
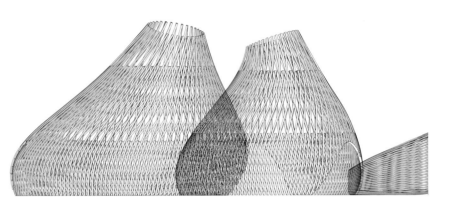

Home/Unusual Store

Venafro, Italy

Architect: Luigi Valente
Year of completion: 2011
Gross floor area: 50 m²
Materials: plasterboards, white plexiglass, neon lights, steel, wood, micro concrete with resin

This clothing store in Venafro, Italy, has an oxymoronic mission: to simultaneously resemble a cozy home and a fantasyland. Conceived as a giant display cabinet, the Home/Unusual Store was designed with a simple color palette and ample display space. Designer Luigi Valente opted for stark black walls that contrast with steel structures and neon white lights, a cold hard aesthetic complemented by the resin that covers the floor and left wall. Each element is conceived, designed and implemented to display the garments in the most eye-catching way possible. Sceptics might say that such an aim is impossible to achieve using grey as the key color, yet Luigi Valente has made splendid use of that underrated color here to create an engaging contemporary space.

and I tha   you
from bring me here

finally I've found
that I belong here

for showing me ho
for singing these t

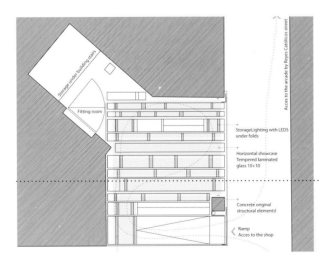

Storage under building stairs

Fitting room

Acces to the arcade by Reyes Católicos street

StorageLighting with LEDS under folds

Horizontal showcase
Tempered laminated glass 10+10

Concrete original structural elementsl

Ramp
Acces to the shop

Horizontal Showcase

Granada, Spain

Architect: Serrano + Baquero Arquitectos
Year of completion: 2010
Gross floor area: 35 m²
Materials: iron and glass

Serrano + Baquero Arquitectos were commissioned to transform a former fragrance store in a shopping arcade in the center of Granada into a clothing store. The unattractive location and poorly lit interior overwhelmed with windows and shutters presented a host of obstacles that demanded careful consideration. The result is a compelling space in which private and public areas become blurred and indistinct and where the essential elements are discovered: exposed cement walls, a brick vault, the concrete ceiling structure and moldings. Choosing to radically strip the existing architecture of all that was unnecessary, the designers opened the door to a new type of fashion store, where a raw, unrefined space provides the backdrop to showcase a collection of highly sophisticated garments.

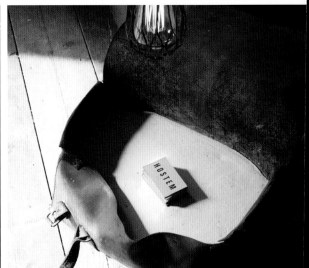

Hostem Shop

London, United Kingdom

Architect: JamesPlumb
Year of completion: 2010
Gross floor area: 186 m²
Materials: wooden floorboards, hessian panels, linen curtains

Walking through the doors of East London menswear store Hostem, the visitor is immediately met with the candle-like glow of the exposed light bulbs overhead. From the solidity of the reclaimed wooden floorboards to the theatrical hand painted and aged wall canvases, the aesthetic is based on a deference to history through the reworking of antique and reclaimed pieces to imbue the present with charm and timelessness. The designers of the store have created a sense of individuality and history, using masterfully reworked mirrors, wood that looks as if it has been pillaged from decades past and simple, honest fabrics to adorn the windows and soft furnishings. Leather railway conductors' bags filled with white concrete display accessories and footwear – details that perfectly frame the beautiful products within.

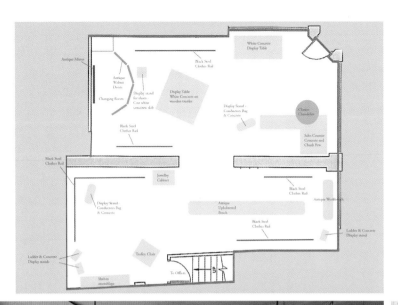

Indulgi

Kyoto, Japan

Architect: Nendo
Year of completion: 2011
Gross floor area: 100 m²
Materials: black wooden floors, soft grey walls with highlights of pink, steel, glass

Aware that an interior can quickly become uninteresting if all of its elements and display products can be seen with a single glance, Nendo decided to add shielding features, creating a space that can never be seen in its entirety, a space in which various elements appear and disappear from view, offering a unique visual experience from every angle. Extra doors have been introduced and set at different angles to control visibility, an addition that also generates a sense of the surreal, inviting the question, "which doors are real and which are fake?" "Fake" doors are used for hangers, shelving and mirrors and furnished with fixtures that spill out from the space beyond in an array of colors and textures, tempting the visitor to open the door and discover yet another new perspective.

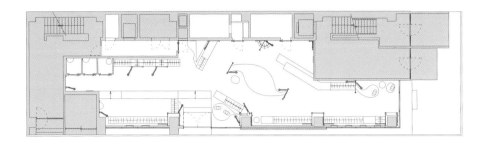

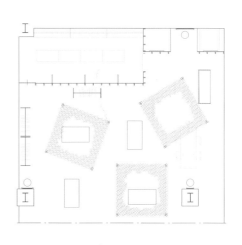

Karis

Hiroshima, Japan

Architect: Suppose Design Office
Year of completion: 2010
Gross floor area: 180 m²
Materials: cardboard tubes, glass and concrete

The space is for shopping but also for holding events. The concept of the store is space that is changing its view or atmosphere depending on where you are standing, such as caves or limestone caves. At some points the place offers a view to the end of the store also of an area surrounded by the inner partitions. The experience walking through the artificial yet random space would be close to something like walking in nature. The purpose of the design is to offer a new shopping experience in which people could see products by strolling in nature.

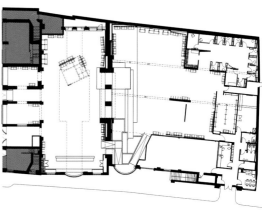

Kings Road Anthropologie

London, United Kingdom

Architect: Anthropologie
Store Design
Year of completion: 2009
Gross floor area: 200 m²
Materials: reclaimed white
oak, fumed finish and garage-
polished concrete (floors);
"wood-cast" concrete tiles
(stairs), walls-artisan plaster

This design transformed an existing street level shop into a dynamic three-story space, woven together with steel, vegetation and light. A light and open monumental stair and 200 square meter living wall respond to the natural light flooding into the store from the skylights over the site. The main steel staircase with cast iron and glass treads reinterprets the monumental stair and allows multiple paths of travel between levels from the front or back of the store. 14 different plant types inhabit the living wall, which stitches the three floors together and was conceived as a whimsical and more organic version of plaid fabric. The "Parlour Room" at the front of the store has a custom concrete tile floor that is a modern interpretation of a traditional wood floor pattern. A steel clad threshold leads into the main sales floor which is dominated by reclaimed white oak, while the basement level walls are finished in plaster impressed with lace and the first floor dazzles in high-gloss white paint.

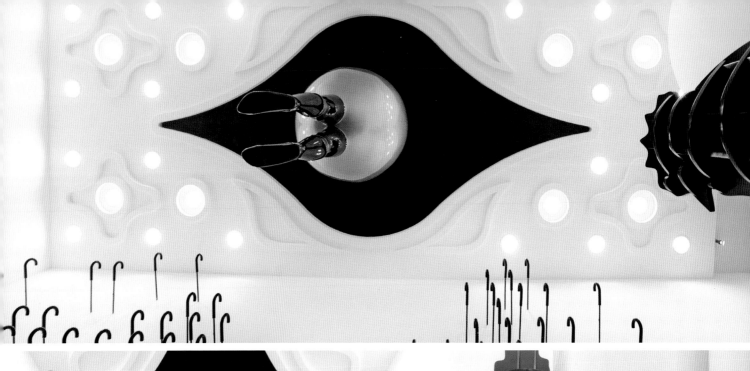

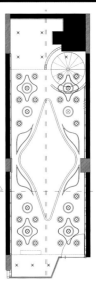

KooKoo

Nicosia, Cyprus

Architect: SuperNova Studio
Year of completion: 2011
Gross floor area: 45 m²
Materials: MDF – board with blue finish, plasterboard, 100 umbrella handles, fiber glass ceiling

The success of the Kookoo boutique lies in its bold and quirky interior which is at once eye-catching and memorable. Striking elements including a giant blue rooster, are visible from the street outside, enticing passersby inside, where those same elements form highly inventive and prominent displays for the products. Faced with a low ceiling, the designers took the bold decision to re-move part of an upper floor to create a partial mezzanine, greatly adding to the sense of space. Umbrella handles protruding from the walls offer a versatile method to display small accessory items. These are cleverly arranged to draw the eye up to the ceiling where a golden egg provides a humorous focal point for the interior, mirroring and distorting the space in its reflective surface.

» **Fashions** fade,
Style is **eternal.** «
Yves Saint Laurent

The Lake & Stars

New York, USA

Architect: SOFTlab
Other creatives: Focus Lighting
Year of completion: 2011
Gross floor area: 167 m²
Materials: black, velvet-covered wall, dichroic plexi-glass

Pushing the boundaries of what a retail space can be, SOFTlab took the reins for the last two weeks at TriBeCa's unique BOFFO Building Fashion space. The New York design studio created a "store within a store" installation that presents a series of highly innovative "view cones" through which visitors can survey the garments displayed behind. With the interior coated in a white, reflective, glossy skin, and the outer clad in soft, black ma-terial, absorbing extraneous light, focused light is thrust through the cones to create a vibrant, human-scale kaleidoscope that enthralls each and every passerby. This cutting-edge installation – a wholly respectable and highly elegant peep show – invites visitors to engage in the visual extravaganza created by the interaction of superbly designed fashion and architecture.

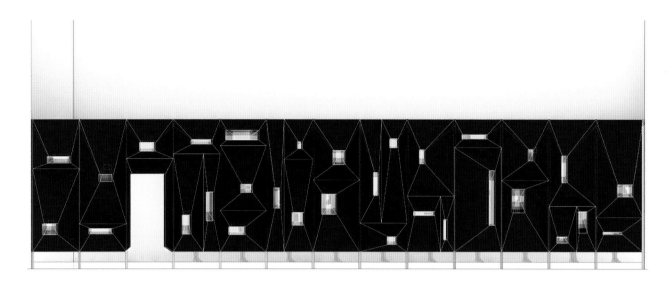

Levi's

Amsterdam, The Netherlands

Architect: Como Park
Year of completion: 2011
Gross floor area: 240 m²
Materials: wood, metals, vintage pieces, found objects, and bycicles: 90% recycled or reclaimed

ReStore: reuse, rebrand, rejuvenate – this is the concept behind the new 240 square meter Levi's store in Amsterdam, a retail space designed to reflect the city itself. Faced with problematic permit regulations, Como Park were forced to re-evaluate their initial design, a fortuitous turn of events that resulted in this highly inventive and vibrant interior. Open, colorful shelving represents the keystone of the design, which manifests passion and humor through its bold aesthetic statements. The lighting and wooden floor from Levi's Bread & Butter stand were reused, while old doors were mounted on vintage church benches to create a display table for denim apparel – old and new are juxtaposed perfectly in this fun and quirky new store.

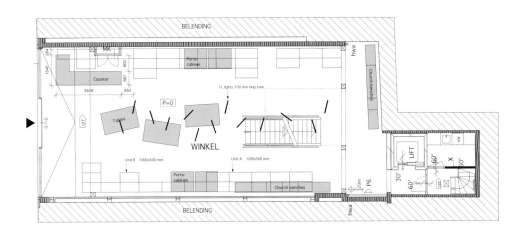

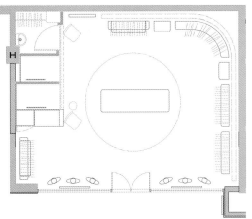

Little Joe Woman

Sydney, Australia

Architect: MAKE Creative
Year of completion: 2011
Gross floor area: 50 m²
Materials: plywood shingles,
fishing nets (black satin)

The Little Joe Woman brand, designed by ex-model Gail Elliott, has its origins in the Hamptons, a heritage reflected in the screen clad in shingles, a striking element that is repeated and reinterpreted in every Little Joe Woman store. This bold new store is housed in an exposed concrete shell with a curved screen of raw plywood shingles wrapping around the space. With their sleek white powder coat finish, the display units act as a refined counterpoint to the surrounding unfinished surfaces, a combination of sophistication and unrefined simplicity that beguiles the visitor. An intriguing light installation above the main sales counter comprises glass spheres suspended inside fishing nets, a simple feature that enhances the unifying urban beach aesthetic.

Lurdes Bergada

Barcelona, Spain

Architect: Dear Design
Year of completion: 2009
Materials: thin smoothed
cement floor, birch plywood
cement and natural
varnished iron

In keeping with the fashion brand's industrial and mini-malistic style, Dear Design created a vast hangar-like feel by including all of the functions of the store – both client facing and back-room – under one roof, but separating them with a curving wall. This wall, created with 1,000 pieces of beech wood held together by 2,400 screws, forms an igloo-like huge presence and becomes a fo-cal point that emphasizes the size of the entire space.

Each piece of wood is unique and each piece is visibly numbered – a necessary technical detail for building the wall and a creative design idea to expose the "making of" and to bring attention to the construction features. The use of concrete, wood and cement further adds to the warehouse-like atmosphere.

the collection for men

Maison Martin Margiela

Maison Martin Margiela

Beijing, China

Architect: Consuelo Castiglioni, in collaboration with Sybarite
Year of completion: 2011
Gross floor area: 540 m²
Materials: glass, raw cement, fluorescent and neon lights, carpet, "parquet" printed linoleum, steel and mirrors

With a surface area of 540 square meters, this two-story boutique is the largest Maison Martin Margiela store in the world. In the window, neon lights outline the striking figure of a woman, drawing the eyes of passersby and enticing them inside where they are greeted by simple clean lines and the iconic white and silver shades of the Maison. Coated in raw cement and adorned with hexagonal fluorescent lights, the ceiling bears the signa-ture of the brand's minimalist style. The collections are housed in uniquely themed and decorated cubes – white curtains and carpet in the women's department, "par-quet" printed linoleum in the men's department and real tiles for the MM6 label. A movable, mirrored changing room on castors inspires a spirit of fun and modernity, while spotlights, neon lights and lamps on racks gener-ate a glow that spreads throughout the store.

Marni Beijing

Beijing, China

Architect: Sybarite
Year of completion: 2011
Gross floor area: 550 m²
Materials: backlit fiber glass boxes, stainless steel rails, velvet-clad seating, wallpaper and carpet of interlocking octagons

A bold black and white motif of interlocking octagons covers the walls of this two-story boutique in Beijing's Sanlitun district. Marni's biggest flagship store in the world, designed by Sybarite, is defined by the interior's powerful geometric focus that unites all of the elements in the 550 square meter space. A cherry-red staircase adds a welcome splash of color to the monochromatic walls, while massive stainless steel rails keep clothing organized, doubling as spectacular fluid sculptural forms. The overtly industrial style of the existing staircase, preserved as a key design feature, contrasts strikingly with the polished sophistication of the rest of the boutique – a bold juxtaposition that challenges the limits of contemporary design.

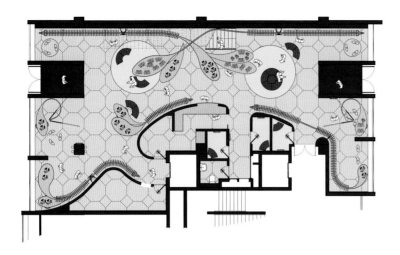

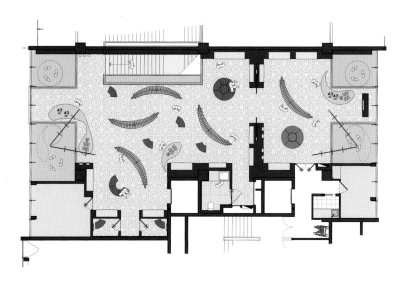

Max Mara Chengdu

Chengdu, China

Architect: Duccio Grassi Architects
Year of completion: 2011
Gross floor area: 720 m²
Materials: wooden walls, copper, glass

Driven by a concept of design that focuses on the people who will use and work in the space – retail workers and customers – Duccio Grassi Architects created a unique interior in which the product is not even visible at first glance. Instead, visitors are attracted by a series of visual stimuli – large cylindrical volumes made of burnished brass and painted white on the inside. Furnished with these volumes, the space offers a fluid ambience that invites the flow of both light and people, provoking a dialogue with the outside world that challenges rigid notions of interior and exterior space. Wood covering on the walls repeats itself apparently infinitely in vertical lines and shadows. This is an interior activated by people – only with their movement and laughter does this place come alive.

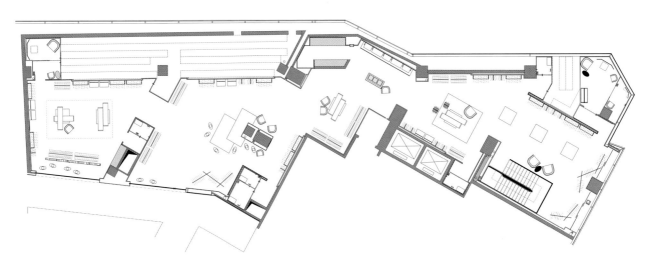

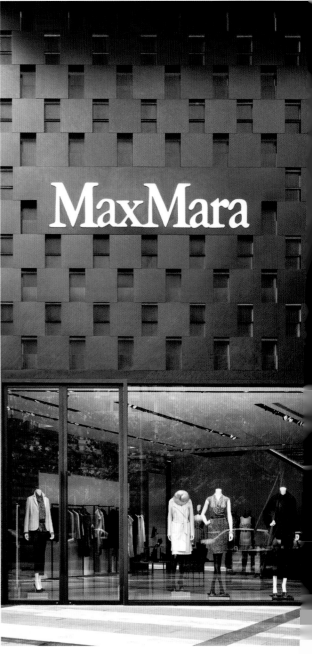

Monki Carnaby Street

London, United Kingdom

Architect: Electric Dreams
Year of completion: 2012
Gross floor area: 450 m²
Materials: merry-go-rounds, tangled ropes, sparkling jellyfish floating, glowing bubbles, mirror surfaces

Launching their third concept design, the Monki architects have created a dazzling underwater world using a khaki-based color scheme, mirror ceiling, silver sparkling lighting and more than 50 custom-made design products. Fascinated by anything that is "too colorful, too weird, too beautiful," the designers used playful exaggeration, spatially confusing mirrors and surprising shapes to create the surreal interior of the store. Clothes hang on tangled ropes from long gone schooners, the mirror ceiling evokes an all-reflecting watery surface, and walls are clad with white metal scales from an ever-present underwater being. Laser-cut water lily tables and tentacled jellyfish sparkling with light complete this bold and bizarre, yet ultimately joyous and inspirational interior.

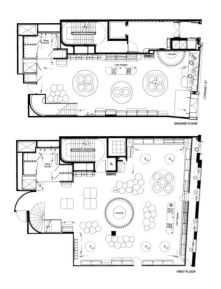

Monospace

Taipei, Taiwan

Architect: Arboit
Year of completion: 2011
Gross floor area: 250 m²
Materials: metal rods, lacquered wood, laminate glass, carpet, epoxy resin

Playfulness meets sophistication in this surprising new retail shop in Taipei. Angular rails jut from the walls, floor and ceiling as display racks for clothes, evoking memories of idyllic days spent on climbing frames in the playgrounds of our childhood. The large monochromatic red space dares visitors to explore the collections creatively and playfully, inviting them to interact with the clothes as a curious child, free from inhibitions. Standard retail space schemes are rejected in favor of a fashion playground where we are invited to believe that anything is possible.

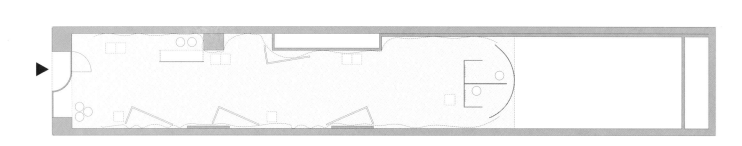

Nanushka Beta Store

Budapest, Hungary

Architect: Daniel Balo, Zsofi Dobos, Dora Medveczky, Judit Emese Konopas and Noemi Varga
Year of completion: 2012
Gross floor area: 80 m²
Materials: billowed canvas canopy and a sliced firewood floor, fabric (walls and ceiling)

Nanushka retail space boldly expresses the brand's core values, offering welcome relief from the sometimes-overwhelming urban experience. A group of handpicked architecture graduates had a small budget and just three short weeks to complete the project. Drawing inspiration from classical wedding tents and rustic barn interiors, they gathered raw materials such as cotton, linen, firewood and rusted steel to use as the basic interior elements, chosen in accordance with the eco-friendly design concept. Canvas was hoisted into the air and allowed to flow and fall freely, appearing to defy gravity, while small display stands built from wooden logs seem to sprout from the ground. Linen poufs and balloon lamps sharing the same cylindrical shape further strengthen the organic flow of the space.

Nature Factory

Tokyo, Japan

Architect: Suppose Design
Office
Year of completion: 2009
Gross floor area: 65 m²
Materials: plastic plumbing
pipe, wooden floors and the
polished cement slab walls

This latest work from Suppose Design Office for the Diesel Denim Gallery in Aoyama, Japan, functions as a gallery space for art installations and exhibits contemporary work throughout the year showcasing talented young artists. Nature Factory is an "innovative art space" comprising a series of pipes branching across the store in all directions. Appearing random at first glance,

the design of this artificial plumbing was carefully conceived to echo a tree's branches growing over an extended period of time. Garments and accessories are arranged among the network of pipes in an evocative and thought-provoking dialogue between contemporary fashion and innovative architecture.

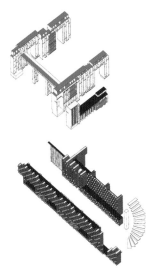

NL = New Luxury

Amsterdam, The Netherlands

Architect: EventArchitectuur
Year of completion: 2009
Gross floor area: 135 m²
Materials: black MDF, plywood

Designed as a space somewhere between a showroom and a shop, New Luxury manifests the personal attention and care given to the garments on display in the architectural display elements themselves. The self-referential spatial system created by EventArchitectuur serves as a container for the garments, treating each as a unique and valuable piece, and at the same time organizes the spaces. A masculine, industrial feel presides in the dark basement, where a spatial system constructed out of black MDF and glass embraces and enhances that darkness. Meanwhile, whitewashed slivers of plywood dominate the ground floor, generating a lighter, more feminine and handcrafted quality.

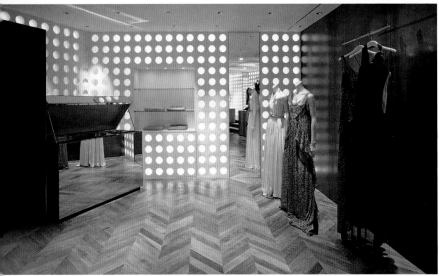

Phillip Lim Boutique

Tokyo, Japan

Architect: Jamo Associates
Year of completion: 2008
Gross floor area: 246 m²
Materials: wood (floor), block (walls)

Asked to design a store that would be both dynamic and romantic, Jamo Associates conceived an interior based around a story titled "in the water," juxtaposing classic and modern elements to reflect Phillip Lim's collections. While an underwater story could easily play out through familiar and obvious design tropes, Jamo interprets this theme subtly through structural elements and decorative details. The interior walls comprise 4,000 "hana-gata blocks," a material used throughout the seaside communities of Okinawa. Brought together, the blocks not only create an aesthetic feeling of air bubbles rising to the ocean's surface but also have functional value in allowing natural light to filter into the space. Custom display fixtures sparkle like treasure chests, while the gradation in color of the shop's oak floors recalls patterns of light and dark, dry and wet sand on a beach.

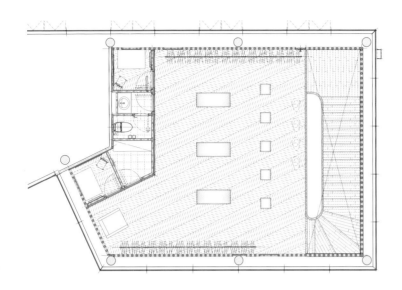

» **Elegance** does not mean
to catch **the eye,**
but to **remain** in the **memory.** «

Giorgio Armani

Ports 1961

Shanghai, China

Architect: Archi-Tectonics
Year of completion: 2011
Gross floor area: 223 m²
Materials: reclaimed wood slats, polished limestone flooring, epoxyed glass fiber, reinforced gypsum

A silvery wood lining forms a tranquil backdrop to the Ports fashion collection in this newly opened store in Shanghai. Suspended over sculpted wooden bases showcasing bags, shoes and jewelry, the garments hang simply, inviting the visitor to linger and to browse. Stepping closer to the wooden structures reveals a surprising secret – the rough outer textures are juxtaposed with a pearly, silvery finish inside generating a warm glow that radiates throughout the store interior. Mannequins suspend the collection in space, which, lit from below by recessed lighting, accentuate the fluidity of the fashion pieces. Movement from visitors causes these mannequins to turn slowly, enhancing the sense of fluidity and creating a mesmerizing effect that hypnotizes and soothes the onlooker.

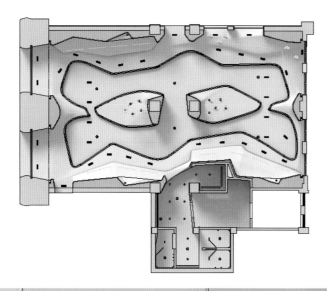

Puma Store

Amsterdam, The Netherlands

Architect: plajer & franz studio
Year of completion: 2012
Gross floor area: 326 m²
Materials: brick walls, wood, HIT lights

Sportswear brand Puma has redesigned and reopened its Amsterdam shop, using its "Retail 2.0" philosophy that fuses shopping and technology in a space that combines innovation, simplicity and vibrancy with key local influences. At the main entrance, Puma cat sculptures offer photo-taking opportunities, while a red Puma "UnSmart Phone" rings as customers approach, offering trivia about Puma. Changing rooms are decorated with blue and white tiles reflective of traditional Dutch Delftware porcelain – a nod to local heritage juxtaposed audaciously with a "Puma peepshow," a red box positioned on a wall that opens to show video clips. Surprising features and technological innovation are met with at every turn, offering each new visitor an engaging and unforgettable retail experience.

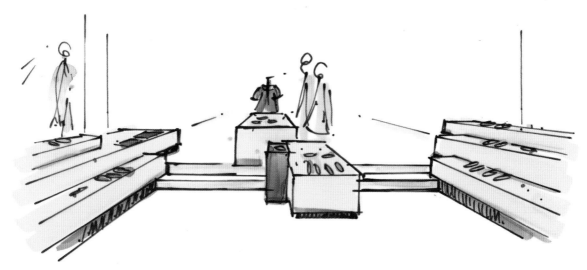

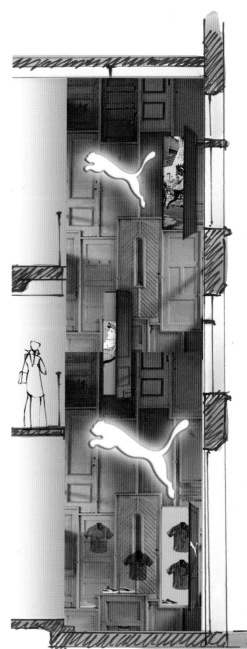

Replay Flagship Store

Milan, Italy

Architect: Studio 10
Year of completion: 2010
Gross floor area: 950 m²
Materials: green wall, water wall, wood, steel

Seeking to create an island, both physical and psychological, within the urban context, Studio 10 designed an internal garden, a vast organic space that welcomes passersby, offering shelter and respite from the city. Monumental walls of plants surround the visitor, while an intoxicating waterfall runs the entire length of the store. These visual and tactile elements were conceived as the starting point from which to build, or rather rebuild, the lost relationship between man and the natural world: the senses are engaged and the mind refreshed. A suspended walkway leads to the main retail space where natural wood and manmade steel combine harmoniously as the dominant materials. A vast wall of denim displays an array of garments, celebrating the craft traditions that provide the brand's inspiration.

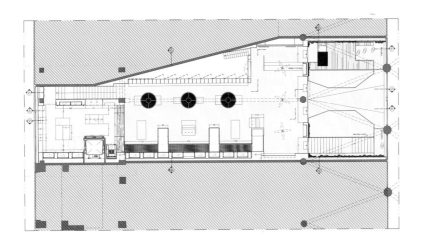

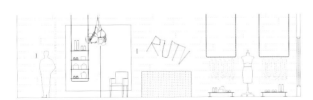
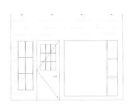
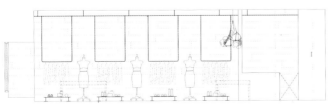
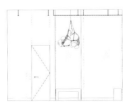

Ruti Boutique

San Francisco, USA

Interior designer: Nicole Hollis
Year of completion: 2011
Gross floor area: 51 m²
Materials: pine barn siding reclaimed wood (walls), concrete (floors), steel rods, acrylic, ceramic tile

Working with a palette of natural materials, most notably wood, Hollis created a backdrop that would not only complement the casual yct highly crafted clothing, but also reinforce the aesthetic of the emerging brand, described by Ruti Zisser as "simple, clean, with attitude." The cool gray tone of the wood with its unfinished, weathered texture alludes to San Francisco's cool, foggy climate and harmonizes with Ruti's desert-inspired gar-

ments. Installed in horizontal bands from floor to ceiling, the material produces a surprisingly elegant effect, while its rough appearance creates a striking foil for the delicate textile creations. Simplicity guided the design of each store element, from the minimalist display and lighting system to the innovative merchandising table created from reams of stacked white office paper.

Shine Fashion Store

Hong Kong, China

Architect: NC Design &
Architecture (NCDA)
Other creatives: World Shine
Lighting, KL & Associates
Construction
Year of completion: 2011
Materials: wood, stainless
steel, leather, granite, mirrors

Asked to design an interior that would reinforce Shine's identity as an avant-garde and experimental fashion store, NC Design & Architecture constructed a seven meter high, asymmetrical, glowing star-like structure that cannot fail to attract the attention of passersby. The pristine white shell encloses a black interior wall that unfolds dramatically to form a suspended staircase leading to the upper sales area. A row of geometrically arranged fluorescent lights above the stairs emits a futuristic, sci-fi glow evocative of the progressive clothing collections on display. A continuously folded kalaidoscopic mirror partition conceals the leather-padded fitting rooms – inspired by music videos and computer generated effects – and cashier entrances in the shop's most intimate area. This visually striking yet highly functional contemporary store is a triumph in modern boutique design.

Siki Im Concept Store

New York, USA

Architect: Leong Leong
Year of completion: 2010
Materials: wood framing and spray foam insulation

Soft Brutalism, the concept store for Siki Im, was developed in collaboration with the fashion designer himself. The concept explores the transformation of an existing space through the insertion of a foreign figure or shape. The structure, which is the former sales trailer for the HL23 building designed by Neil Denari, is filled end to end with a large ramp-form that creates an unexpected gathering space with undefined programmatic possibilities. Soy-based spray foam is used to cover the interior and exterior of the structure creating a supple surface for inhabitation on which visitors are required to remove their shoes. Small niches and ledges are carved into the foam to create areas for display and seating.

Stills Flagship Store

Amsterdam, The Netherlands

Architect: Doepel Strijkers
Year of completion: 2011
Gross floor area: 188 m²
Materials: wooden slats, glass and mirrors

The flagship store for Stills on the Cornelis Schuijtstraat in Amsterdam aims for, and achieves, the height of sophistication through novel combinations and delicate contrasts in fits, styles, looks and feels. Focusing on the intrinsic qualities of materials, the designers created a unique spatial identity defined by refined textures, enthralling patterns and layered volumes. Dressing rooms,

lighting and all conceivable options for presentation are integrated into the white volume – even the clothing, shoes and bags seem to exist as visual continuations of the spectacular structure. Elements of the original building can be glimpsed at various angles, generating a destabilizing sense of timelessness matched only by the disruption of spatial norms that overwhelms the visitor.

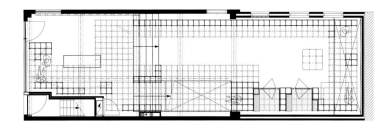

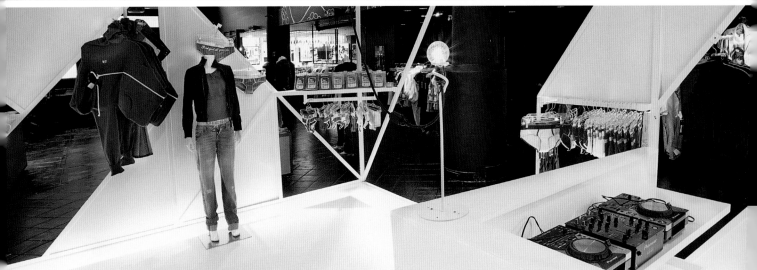

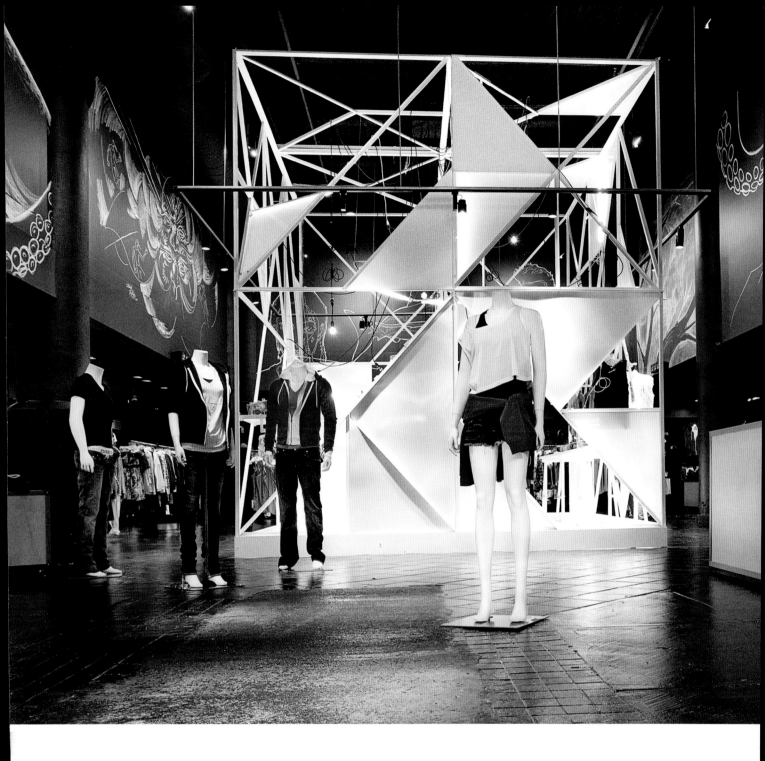

Stylexchange

Montreal, Canada

Architect: Sid Lee Architecture
Year of completion: 2011
Materials: patchwork of concrete, metals, recycled mix materials, painted with black epoxy (floor); gypsum and painted blackboard (wall); concrete (ceiling)

Located adjacent to a university campus in downtown Montreal, this boutique blends seamlessly with the urban landscape of the multicultural neighborhood. The simple and flexible design showcases Stylexchange's contemporary fashions, while also acknowledging and commemorating local history and tradition. A black area displaying new products was conceived as a creative canvas of blackboards, which local artists are invited to decorate in a constantly evolving design. The central workshop is bright and white, focusing the curious visitor's attention on the work of the in-store stylist, constantly at work fashioning new outfits and combinations. Original floors were preserved and feature a diverse selection of tiles from different eras.

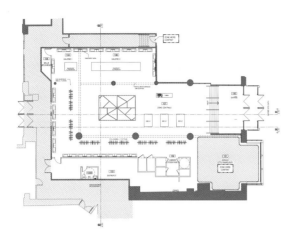

Sunrise

Amsterdam, The Netherlands

Architect: Bearandbunny
Year of completion: 2011
Gross floor area: 360 m²
Materials: white marble, wood, glass

Inspired by the colors of each new day's sunrise, the interior of this "shop as a house" was painted white, a neutral color that reflects and complements the array of colors expressed by the objects and people inside the store. A cabinet full of clothes and a white marble desk greet each visitor as they enter. The furniture is constructed simply out of wooden sticks, painted white and standing in front of a wall with natural oak vitrines positioned symmetrically. A glass house at the back boasts a painted glass ceiling and a host of hanging plants. Taking center stage throughout the interior, the sun is welcomed in through the numerous windows and openings that punctuate this impressive and unique four-story design.

TIPS Fashion Store

Shanghai, China

Architect: ///byn
Year of completion: 2010
Gross floor area: 105 m²
Materials: original wood
floors, stainless steel

This understated fashion store is located on the ground floor of an old French mansion in the heart of the former French Concession of Shanghai. Inspired by the historic residential environment, the designers chose to protect and display the existing architectural details – woodwork, moldings, fire places, beams – as glorious relics of this area's rich history. Contemporary elements have been carefully introduced into this historical framework, acting as counterparts rather than challenges to the original features. A sequence of freestanding bodies composed of a series of pods hold the hanging units and offer storage capacity. The space is transformed by the intriguing geometry of these innovative pods and the connections between them.

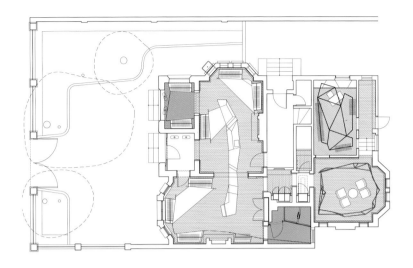

Twister

London, United Kingdom

Architect: 42 Architects
Year of completion: 2010
Gross floor area: 250 m²
Materials: black rubber pipe with a plastic and aluminum core, welded steel bases (benches and tables), MDF wood (table tops)

Twister is a stunning spatial installation designed for Topshop's AW 11 press event in London by Johan Berglund of London-based 42 architects. Conceived, designed and created in just three weeks, Twister proposes an innovative spatial configuration built of intoxicating swirls, swooshes, vortexes and eddies, manifested as a system of hand-formed black PVC coated tubes on which garments are hung. Visitors are invited to follow the structure as it winds enticingly through the room, binding various collections and concentrations of garments together into a single aesthetic whole. A second structural layer of white benches and tables nestles around the tubes, acting both as seats and as surfaces for displaying accessories and shoes. This is architecture at its most dynamic and provocative.

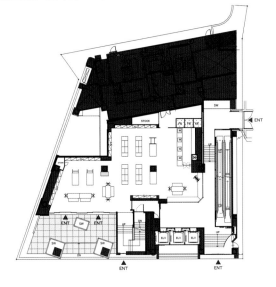

Uniqlo Megastore
Tokyo, Japan

Architect: Gwanael Nicolas / CURIOSITY
Year of completion: 2009
Materials: glass floor, mirrored aluminum and ceramic tiles

The new Uniqlo Megastore adds a civic dimension to its commercial purpose. The vertical displays of the entrance are reflected on the mirrored wall creating an amazing gallery of displays, a maze of reflections of reflections, the tower seeming to be inserted within the interior of the shop. The challenge of the interior is for it not to "exist." Only the clothes should be visible. Display furniture is not only reduced to the minimum but also "designed" to be non-existent with materials selected for their immateriality. A lighting ceiling, displays and counters work together to remove the shadows, creating an abstract retail environment where products and customers seem to float in a white glow.

Zara Flagship Store

Rome, Italy

Architect: Duccio Grassi Architects
Year of completion: 2010
Gross floor area: 5,000 m²
Materials: steel supports and columns, wood

A new Zara flagship store has opened on Via del Corso in Rome, housed in the Palazzo Bocconi, a historic building with a vast and stunning atrium at its heart. Departing from the circular gesture of the atrium cut-out, the ambitious redesign circulates around the central space with the escalators and stair access stacked along the eastern wall. A double skin of perforated panels disguises the building's inner layout while still cleverly allowing natural light to penetrate. At night, the store glows from the inside like a lantern, showcasing the "hung curtain" effect of the perforation and revealing tantalizing glimpses of the interior life of the store. Sustainability was a high priority and this innovative design sets a new standard in eco-efficiency.

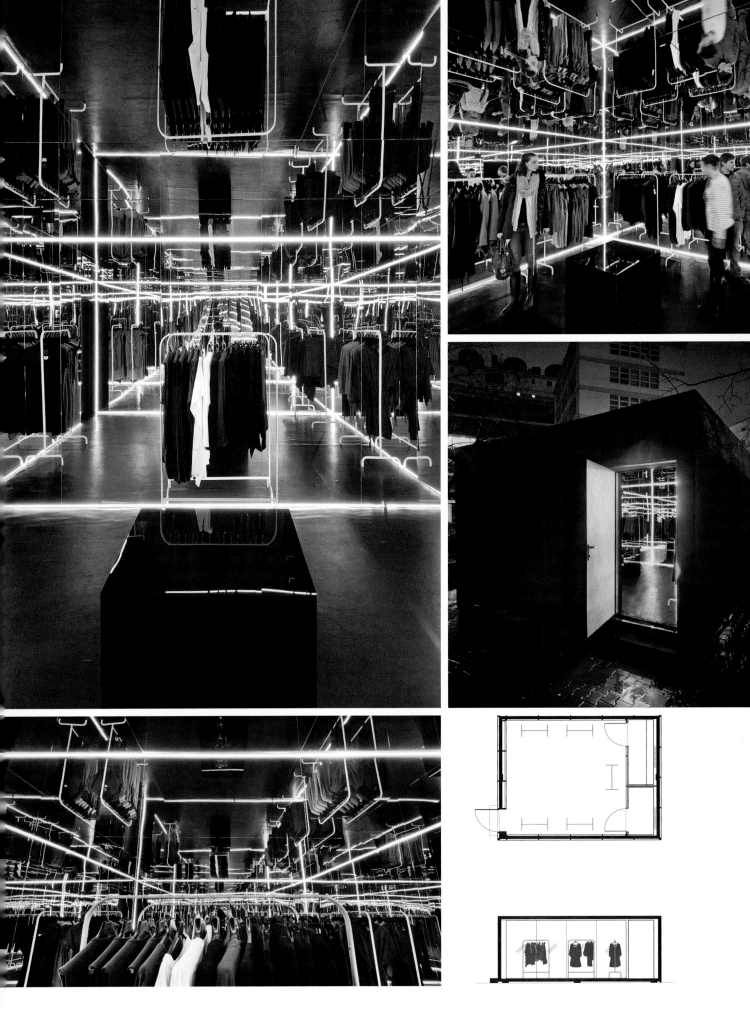

Zuo Corp, Pop-up Shop

Warsaw, Poland

Architect: Super Super and Inside/Outside
Year of completion: 2010
Gross floor area: 27 m²
Materials: office container, mirrors, LED lighting, black canvas

This temporary pavilion for clothing retailer Zuo Corp is the impressive result of collaboration between Polish architects Super Super and Inside/Outside. Mirrors line the ceilings and walls of the tiny pop-up-clothing shop in Warsaw, generating the disorienting illusion of endless rails of garments. Lengths of LED lighting surround the edges of the walls and are reflected in the mirrors – part of an infinite illuminated grid that dazzles and astounds.

Presented from the outside with a simple black cube, visitors are unprepared for the "Alice in Wonderland" experience awaiting them. This design is a true testament to the limitless power of the human imagination when faced with a miniscule space and a budget to match.

Index

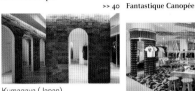

Index Architects

Photo Credits

Javier Callejas Sevilla	82–83
Michel Denancé	74–77
Achim Hatzius	62–63
Jonathan Leijonhufvud	112–117
Courtesy Marni	118–121
Panagiotis Mina	96–97
Rafael Vargas	70–73
42 Architects	180–181
Daici Ano	88–91
Anthropologie Store Design, USA	94–95
Arboit	130–131
Stefan Bauer, www.ferras.at/wikimedia commons, user: Ferras	15 r.
Bearandbunny	172–175
Ali Bekman	28–29
Tamas Bujnovszky	132–133
Tamas Bujnovszky	36–39
Himanshu Chowdhry	42–43
Courtesy Cornet	40–41
Pol Cucala	110–111
Dennis Lo Photography	160–161
Dieguez Fridman	30–31
Peter Duhon/wikimedia commons, user: Mick Stephenson	10
Cosmin Dragomir	48–51
Duccio Grassi Architects	122–125
FABRICA/United Colors of Benetton	15 l.
Courtesy Folk Clothing	64–65
Courtesy Hostem	84–87
© illustrart - Fotolia.com	98
Courtesy inditex	12 b., 184–187
Peter Janczik and Reich und Wamser	54–55
Zowie Jannink	104–107
Evan Joseph	100 a., 102–103
© Tobias Kromke - Fotolia.com	16
Jacek Majewski	188–189
© Pavel Losevsky - Fotolia.com	144
Vinay Mathias	42–43
Shannon McGrath	56–59
Nacása & Partners	18–21
Nacása & Partners	182–183
Nicole Hollis	158–159
Takumi Ota	46–47
© Claudia Otte - Fotolia.com	52
Francesco Pato	34–35
Stefano Pedretti	78–81
Assaf Pinchuk	44–45
plajer & franz studio	150–153
Courtesy Billy Poh & Paul Coudamy	60–61
Process5 Design	32–33
Shen Qiang	24–27
Luc Remond	108–109
Pietro Savorelli	154–157
ken schluchtmann/diephotodesigner.de	66–69
Johannes Schwartz	138–139
Senior Airman Andrea Salazar (U.S. Armed Forces)/ wikimedia commons, user: Officer	12 a.
Sid Lee	168–171
David B. Smith	162–163
Frederik Sweger	126–129
Kozo Takayama	140–143
Alan Tansey	100 b.
Wouter vandenBrink	164–167
Toshiyuki Yano / Nacása & Partners	134–137
Toshiyuki Yano	22–23
Toshiyuki Yano / Nacása & Partners	92–93
Jiang Yong	146–149
JIANG Yong ///byn	176–179

Cover: from left to right, from above to below:
Courtesy Marni, Luc Remond, © Gina Smith – Fotolia.com,
Assaf Pinchuk, Evan Joseph
Backcover: Dennis Lo Photography

All other pictures, especially plans, were made available
by the architects/designers.